SUPER

NATURAL

SUPER

NATURAL

by
Tracey McTague

SUPER NATURAL by Tracey McTague
Published by Trembling Pillow Press
New Orleans, LA
ISBN-13: 978-0-9887257-0-6
Copyright © Tracey McTague

All Rights Reserved. No part of this book may be reproduced in any form without permission from the publisher with the exception of brief passages cited or for educational purposes. Reproduction for commercial use is prohibitedexcept by permission of the author.

Typesetting and Design: Megan Burns
Cover Art: Mother's wrist xray mudra © Tracey McTague
Cover Design: Unsinkable Design

Trembling
Pillow
PRESS

For Aurora Morrigan

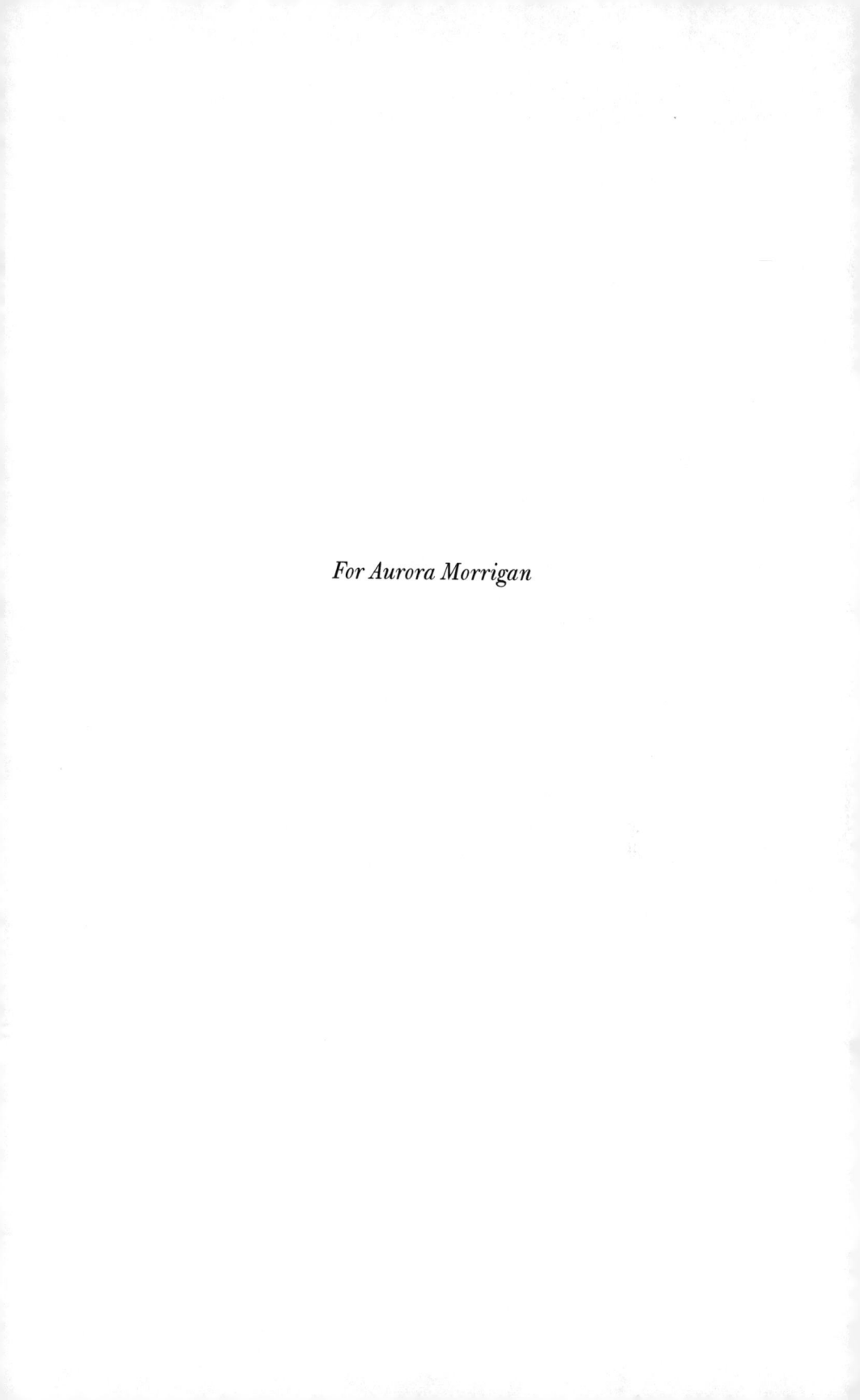

Contents

THIRST

gem spa splashometer	17
Liber Lucis	18
astral rejection	19
'tis my ruin	20
quid pro bro	22
Jim B's junk fish	23
owl estate farming	25
petit a rex reach	26
queen without a face	27
port of call's last call	29
mors osculi (in the Little Office of Virgins)	30
half man half snack	33
thee	34
robot squat	37
stand down dark bird!	38
nostos swoop	39
"Pome"	42
Guernica Botanica	43
Common apotropaic amulets worn for protection from the evil eye	44
Saint Zita's Kobayashi Maru	45
mother tongue fin mot	46

ANCESTOR MIDDEN

Missisippi banned the weeping veil	50
you're an adagio	51
Leather Daddy Pond	52
slightly off hand	53
Kármán vortex street	54
step it down	55
secondhand owl	56
Tenebrosi	57
melancholia fumosa	58
omelet with Alice	59
pas de deux auditions	61
passé partout	62

Inari meat jasmine	63
customs for dead saints	64
fox bones of courtiers	65
lobbed roar	67
Grand Master van Rensselaer	68
mossbonkers	69
blackeye vs. monicle	70
DB Cooper Valentine	71
Ostreidae crassostrea virginica	74
No Rabbits Just Hats	75
reckoner rapture in resuscitation bay	76
idyll deal	77
mall everlasting	78
Water of Fail	79
Blowhole Blowhole give me back my cow	81
in memoriam, for David	83
through hearing in the Bardo	83
idyll of indigenous expressions	84

CONTAGION

Ars longa, vita brevis, occasio praeceps, experimentum periculosum iudicium difficile	90
cotillion contagion	91
trick day	92
she who whispers	93
is a chaos	94
on the run	95
Saint Expedite	96
this was a person it seems	97
above anemones	98
goods unlimited	100
falsely entitled soccer fans	101
traiteuse	102
Dem Tod ein Paar Schuhe schenken	105
Scalapino vs. Barbarino	106
aqua e sali	108
ladyboy lullaby	109
book of whore hours	110
unctuous decline	112
Incunabula	113

Ein Sof Ayin 114
double secret probation 115

Drala

"In Tibetan, a magical quality of existence is called drala: *dra* means "enemy" or "opponent" and *la* means "above."

When we draw down the power and depth of vastness into a single perception, then we are discovering and invoking magic. By magic we do not mean unnatural power over the phenomenal world, but rather the discovery of innate or primordial wisdom in the world as it is. Drala is the unconditioned wisdom and power of the world that are beyond any dualism; therefore drala is above any enemy or conflict…

…There is no fundamental separation or duality between you and your world. When you can experience those two things together, as one, so to speak, then you have access to tremendous vision and power in the world - you find that they are inherently connected to your own vision, your own being. That is discovering magic…"

- *Chögyam Trungpa*

PART I

THIRST

*On the back
of various ancient apotropaic amulets
there inscribed the two words: "I drink."*

*The evil eye is thought to cause a withering sickness;
women and cows lose milk, crops dry out and babies die of thirst.
Life depends upon liquid; milk, blood, semen, saliva and the like.*

*Evil eye belief develops where there is a disparity of wealth distribution
and therefore the social flow of sexual rights.
This is the concept of "limited good."
If someone has a lot,
someone else doesn't have enough.*

Super Natural 16

gem spa splashometer

apprentice yourself to prey
lingered ecstasies enfold
& descend to other
forecast foreboding

embody expanded sense
to travel in mind abundantly
backbone slips with hands on hips

*"I know that place
it stalks me."*

forgetting of the air
visible and the flesh
reciprocate vestigial
vowel moaned more true

Liber Lucis

merely painted but
beautifully incoherent
panegyric to logos

milky way wades
in so many willing ears
nursing trickster or fanatic
fervor enters bouncy castle provinces

essence of arsenic
for dwelling domestic
with townie innovations

diabolical splendor
elixir possessed
by Exorcist sequels
swig Burton's bourbon
to speak bird

flight foretold in future
virgin's milk fluent
in dialect of lusting angels

astral rejection

"fichu comme l'as de pique"

mysterium of the bird-headed bitch
plunderfun thou against me
to devour or be devoured
flame still within
unseen archer pierces himself
despair envoys dispatched
dubious poet archetype
I've killed better men with much smaller guns

vault of cave contains
rapture of self lost
flint work roused
stone age déjà vu
immensity beyond shroud of food
vanished animal vanquished
only half untrue but unforgotten
not in entire   forget fullness
in a trance
insect as god
to & fro
above all
insensate

'tis my ruin

for Friday Jones

quickening
makes the name
spell producing a world
animate kick ass
at birth gods falter
waking perceivable present
graying out into limitless

basic melody echoes
from whence anchor
mind rides spirit
cupped in hand
water there
to sing backward

In southern Italy it is customary to follow any compliment of an infant with a criticism, such as, "How pretty, oh, but look, she has a little dirt on her chin." If the compliment is not balanced in this way, the mother will spit on her child to remove the bad eye.

quid pro bro

disrupted   yo
concealed sublime
to befall grasp

a bird
yet nothing
he already knows
fights reflection
not by reaching

Antigone brand condoms
voids order bluff
of phantom-limb aces
up sleeve giving back
your own hand

Jim B's junk fish

sentient breath
converges between lungs
glazed by wear
& beckons conjuror
in star filter swoop
distinct modalities
stretch and flex of wings
remembering inert
humming descent
of carnal chirp
peacock feather
removes gaze
open ended ending
heretical choir shuts up
singing in drunken reverb
hardly speech at all

*The word 'envy' is etymologically derived from the Latin 'invidere':
to see or seeing.*

owl estate farming

after Brett Evans

whole owl
holy smoke
snare events why not
await apparition armor
of fate's detour amour
still alive only because
she forgot she was dead
with time to kill
& retroactive opinion's
eclipse renounced
by so-called eyes

thangka Zippos
generate flame
vanishing in points
present shift
lucid in flesh
darkening lip thick sky
black cloud beckons
broken gleaning
sun & wing folded up
for miscellaneous business
of so-called living

petit a rex reach

palpate your god particles
mass backwards MacGuffin
play of lights out
in said blossoms
assassin of liberation
consumed with words
carnal stars thy symptom
utterly annihilated
massive aspect of look
lends seeing into
unlearned fate region
fibre by fibre
myriad of fire within

queen without a face

your tromp l'oeil taxed the eye
with mother-of-pearl rapture
as obligatory lutes swelled
her ability to molt
instantly at will
undone by drink
that messy messenger of gods
& guide of the dead
splendid protector of gamblers
liars and thieves

'Tip' comes from the old English word 'tipple' meaning to drink liquids as a means of averting the evil eye, a curse that often takes the form of wasting or drying out. The current practice of tipping emerged as a symbolic means of equalizing the relationship between the drinker and server. A good tip means the server won't be envious of the served, envy being the primary means of inadvertently transmitting the evil eye.

port of call's last call

2nd avenue service
to minor planetoids
infinitely delayed

lose a tooth for every child
ultimate fighter ultimately loses all teeth
tattoo of serpent vs. eagle vs. tiger
battle royale cuts your nose
to spite your face off
ape a grin for bird-ally's
clipped wings and lost causes
not exactly up

fatal flaw steeped
in souvenir of slack
heart spur on the heel sleeve
scuttles ship from sky

the ant carried the decapitated ant head
so matter of factly
the normalcy of circus music
& things like thirst

mors osculi (in the Little Office of Virgins)

for John Coletti

I beseech thee o undefiled one
your unbound litany of winged dog
bruised diversions offer
rays from open eyes
and wounds the thing beheld
expulsion of half cocked crown
by boundary mitzvah
animarum venator gone wild
she who has ears flirts & weeps
synchronistic & in dwelling
revives cowrie mundi
& fire bird Coletti
that iridescent corvid
electro magnetic feathers'
ultra violet instincts
prism-trick such light aquiver
pierced & refracted rite
shimmers a coarser eye aloft
o heresy of flying ceaselessly!
exile every humble blade of grass
a sorceress in sweet depravity
& general decay
you lovely vulgar thing

hortus conclusus

"...a song is the exultation of the mind dwelling on eternal things, bursting forth in the voice."
-Thomas Aquinas

"I'm not sure, but I think all music came from New Orleans."
-Ernie K. Doe

O eye & lamp
where are we?
macula witness
bestow ripeness
broken into atoms
feathers back into wing
give ear to telepathic eye
seized unseen
weaving wanting
beholder eye
in root depravity
trees abandoned
for rhizome wanderer
sly auger one of the fates
still on the lamb

Spinnbarkeit

"The widespread belief that hunters, warriors, or athletes should avoid sex is very likely related to the notion that a man's [power]… may be siphoned by the female genitals."

-Alan Dundes, *Wet and Dry Evil Eye*

The cervical fluid of women changes consistency throughout the cycle and plays a vital role in fertilization. Cervical fluid becomes abundant, clear, and stretchable, like egg white. Before ovulation, this potent stretchy substance maintains the survival of sperm inside the woman's body for many days. The stretchability of the fluid is described by it's spinnbarkeit, from the German word for the ability to be spun. Only such stretchy fluid can be penetrated by sperm. After ovulation it changes consistency and sperm cannot penetrate it.

half man half snack

memory's art of
on the mount
brain fog tidings
tumbling twain
thirsts ensue
& warms true
ambrosia drowning
nigh blindly
to discern
elation befoged
in dynamis dead end

fits of prophecy
throne in head possessed
of divine blasphemy
& bestial belated hope
peacock feathers dipped in
gold invocation

pestle of dying ocean's
gleaming egg adrift
adorns contaminant
such a rarefied brute
full of reckless grace

lavish miniatures
of illuminated full frontal boy choirs
forbidden feasts
roaming in secret trials
of our grubby nocturnal hearts
wink twice if you want
to be saved

thee

holy daff spirit
dawn of possessed sight
sacred deviant beset with
restless light   reign without bond
sea of chop from living water
magnificent toe-bells
ruling blaze inward
cup on fire   glow in gloaming
to perish but awake evermore

*The English word sick comes from the Latin siccus
which means "dry".*

Fitzroy Fatcap

veiless gold dawn risen before
silkworm's rising unwound

sea swallowed up whole
carves luminous boundaries
dreamed in half-light anima
wife with sex removed
lead with your tongue
& hideous holy hunger
visionary fuck ups fucking
with iridescent crow's
rainbow wing-grease

defiled definitions
bleary & strident
those blathering dullards
wait for another pint
to snake past genital logic
of Luna moth's, "Look Ma, no mouth!"

ghost child unafraid
of maggot prism
in lichen shadow
of headstone copse
replete with nudie magazines
tarot cards & dirty jokes

tongue in cheek
germ in this
nowhere for us
jump through twilight's
dissembled time
version of future if

robot squat

for Brad Will

wild eyes ache
as black ink shines
in green sea's
swirling debris
below bright undertow
of invasive nest's
wing-tossed sky

the largesse of multitudes
get the shakes on
for a real bender
naming the night
unbridled & rising
spell of corvid's skull
ascent with song

what's left   to say   anyway
in Mid-City   a boatload   illuminated
in straight jacket   smile

stand down dark bird!

frost bound
dear head walled
in echo light
this loud heart's clamor
for priest & slave sippy cup
oscillates undecided

bioluminescence
holy ghost equivalent
descends to mend
pez filled proposals
abandoned blaze
& deep sea eloped gaze
into salvation schicker night's
end this Elysium dream monger

eremite ablutions
sea-eye project
jelly fish mimics
periodic flash of light
for a hag's eggy slime

pale flower's court appearance
moon vapor buyback
shot of damp breath neat
& baser pant beat
diffuse & mimic
to revisit lips & obscene ravens

hope-wormed contagion
born darkly
but fearfully afar
exquisitely miserable
burst lung forth
to write under water more

nostos swoop

*...Sing to me of the man, Muse, the man of twists and turns
driven time and again off course, once he had plundered the hallowed
heights...*

too hot the eye shines
but too numb to worry
as well-washed nun whispers
"Get thee to a summary of want."

gray glance invokes wink
108 hollow ships
sleep in your halls
weft vs. warp
unraveled night shift
under shrouded
low-tide's grotto slime
cawed catcalls for Calypso
pealing bells bottomed
out of the cage
Mr. Feathers' raptor vector
on the wing & up in the air
lead wild things to their doom

Poughkeepsie keepsakes
& forgotten namesakes
pulled loose loop by loop
woof cup's bottoms up
threadbare shadows
for tomb vandals tag up
sfumato provenance
ignites weave while out
invisible scenes seen in web

nymph detainment center
calls Minoan hot line
a tryst wrist kiss
on the pulse

& tropos tip cup
last instar emerges
after take off

A Toast

Claude Lévi-Strauss describes the rules governing liquids among Indo-European and Semitic people. The notion of limited good requires one to offer beverages to others. When people toast your health with a drink, they are saying, "I drink, but not at your expense. I am replenishing my liquid supply but I wish no loss of yours." This is part of why people feel it is bad luck to toast around someone who is not participating in the toast.

"Pome"

for Kevin Mitchell

o sum game
darling backlash
no bones about it
it's a schlemiel reveal
for doomsday rorschachs'
inconsolable inky tongue

glitter entropy's
sideshow for Southie savages
(just so you know: your mom wants you to do it)
show me your fog castle
lady baboon   with your birds all about
waxing idiots tip werewolves poorly
like red capes for bulls seeing red
we skip to the story's end
for semper fi sturgeon
no mas no poco stowed below

chocolate mingle turn-ons
at herpes camp calling
the kettle black
o wicked pot!

Guernica Botanica

for Alliah Humber

hydraulic lick
more lure less hook
dose of grandiose
leaves gem crust on phantom limb
impastoed gauze of haze
around lake helix
mitigating mandalas &
dénouement repent bent

Tokyo "Little Boy" debris
caught in mobius moustache
animatronic eyes on
your indentured conceit
slit tilt pantie war's
frayed delay

my hardcore Kouros
bares archaic smile for
contrapposto's
getting a leg up

Common apotropaic amulets worn for protection from the evil eye

hunchback
anchor
crescent moon
fish
eye
horse shoe
scissors
horn
fig
hand

Saint Zita's Kobayashi Maru

no win win-win
cleaves saintly cleavage
& bread borrowed
for botanical lie

Ro-ro's tutu too pink
jettatura's schlock sum
in parlor afterlife
inscrutability perfected
by wretched damsels
more bonobo (under the skirt)
amor heroes contagions
transfixed in ruckus excess
uncorrupted

Jovian ministry privy
to last luteal prank
circe charms the best ruse
infinity vs. zero

triple   option   wishbone
in play   all over nothing
a gaping   whole   take me with you

impulse transmitter's snug menace
in the pants a palindrome
of lemniscate stealing mirth

mother tongue fin mot

for Karen Weiser

raven extonare
thunderstruck by
inscrutable garuda
court Krispie pre-K
my child's ¼ usury & ¾ drunk

pocus hope wagging
tail of locus lust
muon to a gluon
promises to lie
tuber clone on the run
patois unwritten in the thick
of it   interrupt   with stammer
goosed & radiant mule

bal masque very vichy
Afro-dye-T doubloons
strange particles winnowing time
radical stranger take your pick
add back by harking forward
Anselm's wine colored guts
sifting through storm

tsunami touched ground
on wave train
"I'll wave to you," vis-à-vis
king cake babytalk
epiphany of the gilded bean
trinket under petticoat
lickety-splits

PART II

ANCESTOR MIDDEN

Veneration of the dead is based on the belief that the deceased have a continued existence and possess the ability to influence the fortune of the living. In some Eastern cultures, and in Native American traditions, the goal of ancestor veneration is to ensure the ancestors' continued well-being and positive disposition towards the living and sometimes to ask for assistance. The social and non-religious function of ancestor veneration is to cultivate kinship values and continuity of the lineage.

Midden deposits can contain a variety of archaeological material, including animal bone, shell, botanical material, vermin, and other artifacts and eco-facts associated with past human occupation. Generally, a midden is laid down in deposits as the debris of daily life are tossed on the pile.

Missisippi banned the weeping veil

no thing itself
in mourning
lilac should follow
a widow's weeds
redemption mantle's
naked pixels
under curio cloak
for one use only

you're an adagio

Jules & Jim's
illusion possible
through reveries rolling dice
radical failure
pulling-out-some-of-the-stops

desire is always a desire of a desire
too many ifs
to many impossible forevers

manifest lilies for hobbled mermaids
a flue for flames
in depravity sublime

Leather Daddy Pond

for Arlo & Christa Quint

"Ask Me About 'Nam" button
tricked-out damsel fly circles
pony off the clock
settles a score while scoring
into infinite time & space
the runner had no legs (or feet)
striving outside
into ecstatic non future

isomorph biotch!
time not for nothing
no linear now
opens horizon
stripping air of anima
into homecoming's
irrevocable hatching

slightly off hand

for Brendan Lorber

pictograph porn
of inanimate matings
reciprocate cosmic mouth to mouth
when dying's unified within

impossible to con an honest man
slot machined odds
coming up one bell short
foresee future by a few ticks
adapted from octopus'
inky black surround sound

isolate in color shift
silver lining siege
of sacred offering
on mark down
monsoon soon enough
needing seconds

Kármán vortex street

> *On her deathbed, Doris Duke hallucinated she was in Brooklyn. She could not be convinced otherwise and in her last thoughts, she died there.*

call in an '82'
in flight music
delayed by storm
expired hope
on borrowed time

precisely retro active
this childhood schlock
for count down
in god forsaken somewhere
hitched to everything else

white people's problems
not my problem
drawn up drawbacks
separation of flow
fragrance of madness
on bluff bodies
singing power lines
by the bye

step it down

for Erica Kaufman

"It is a gathering of crows, omens, that animates the artifice."
    -Robert Duncan, *The Opening of the Field*

warnings for stowaways
ripe supplication
& fervent devotion
gettin' it all over

career of applied animism's
demented ritual
unmade liturgies
heed epileptic vision
to swallow tongue
in a fit with spit harness

hey hey in hayloft
a condition of yawning light
bird-herald appears
making a joyful noise
& always pays your debts

secondhand owl

after Brett Evans

1.
break in Brett's hour-old ghosts
& bloody mosquito corpse
pass yon well witness
rely on old gags
for new daddies
blood sport retrofits stair kit

2.
mulet-counjaille
chaired & unmusical
the board was bored
by all things pastoral
oyster guffaw in midden
brine bedded raw
flesh-forked while dancing
petrified fate unwound
starting now

Tenebrosi

for Bernadette Mayer

> *a proportion of whiskey in each cask evaporates annually and is known as the "angels' share".*

shadowists soaked in light
consummate fused divinity
& whisky breath
carried on obedient wings

miracle under her aprons
inchoate in this life
transmission corporeal
beyond revelation

it is said of a chimera
coiled lightning &
nonduality
friction & ice
where question marks
exclaim thunder infinite

melancholia fumosa

for Anselm Berrigan

deploy monkey named Peaches
with opposable thumbs up
for Yurei in between
kabuki shots with courtesan backs
pull strings on Sanskrit sexting
to drown in sacred blood

apothecary's vessel
stolen by coin forger
for gold transmutation
& wild eye ordination

this ghost psyche dissolves into ebb
grafitti's promised arcana on the level
everyday hermit with crayfish pie
bloodless lips in the gloam
loitering pale king in thrall
those who burn know
source of milk's evermore
withered mind and faded cheek
waits and no bird sings

omelet with Alice

getting to 5th base
generally all around
into failed purple
of happier houses admired
discarded matter doesn't matter
late as of late
as if waiting to care
as if where else?
elsewhere happy
bird happily ever
after the bird got out
of his mind the perfect life
"he has the life I want," he says
I say I know
I know

pall overall

for Lauren Ireland

lure of flower
falters & feeds the monkey
who bites the hand
reprieve for a thief
deceived by device
conjurer of T-scale

take shrapnel of bartalk
from carrion flight
over graves' rancor
war widows
tend to wait
adrift and above
parade in the pale
defeated effigy
blue prints for pink slips
& forlorn forfeit
spells their end

rude truths amid chaos
shamelessness never sober
debauched and immodest
coup de grâce for donut sluts
on the take with start-up assassins

vitruvian woman's
raven gestured
referential point
initiates non ape co-op
for flat footed primate swag
such guppy advances
give camo rebuff
to your banal appendage
praise cast in alloy
all my waggled moss

pas de deux auditions

dead men don't bite
to settle a score
veni vidi vici
three words for indecent allegory

swallow a plucked pearl
with irreverence & exuberance
to decode fig politics
she met her end
not with an asp
but a basket of fruit

fawning & impotent
consort fit for a queen
in a time of general longing
a hand both flush & flawed

nymph state painted in
ruin still made more complete
dematerialize in defiance
convinced that twilight was dawn

passé partout

for Stacy Schiff

"The greatest achievement for a woman is to be as seldom as possible spoken of."
   -Thucydides

take refuge
with applauding courtiers
excess of purple

monkey paw knots
clenched in primate sweat
serves as an anchor
slungshot by sailors
end of my rope
one, two, many
improvised weapons

mine eye between
ship and dock
sharp-elbowed &
falsely saddled with vices
of other miscreants

blow your cover
by blowing you
unvarnished & vanquished
on a wretched little boat

purple painted satyrs
and gold garlanded nymphs
all amassed
blow by blow
let it be done

Inari meat jasmine

> *Islamic law defines three types of kinship:*
> *by marriage, blood and milk.*
> *The last is referred to as al-rida'a in Arabic.*

everything true or false
undergarment over looked
by townie junkie
counter charm with crow voyeur's
sweat shop wonders
arbitrary beauty
sent in texts
verboten gotten

birds bust on bat's
knock-off-wings
sublimated gorgon-vag sweat
mother's milk mutually exclusive
stock-in-trade
for fig hand gestation
uncanny seed & general gaze
we all scream for eye schema

customs for dead saints

sympathy for devils'
censored side note
pre funeral she-ass milk
& blood on your saddle
such perishable unmentionables
leave threshing floor offerings
in wheat defiled landscape
for H.R. department emoticon
not so resourceful or human

fox bones of courtiers

for Alice Notley

release your most precious thing
on maiden graves melted to shade
clip the wings unwoven
to remove eyes at will
serpent tongue's succubi smile
emptied air from floating world
with strumpet currency

nine foxes
far too much tail
translates whore & soldier's
name on rice
(grain fucked us all)

androgynous amulet
of soapland Sisyphus
martyrs' blood
trembles over veins of gold
bear the faithful's promise
in the holy goblet of plastic
stepping out or into enemies
under water or underfoot
evanescent pearl diver promises
a mocking bird's return

insulate with overhaul
conquest of snakes
& babywrist lingerie
lust buffered with tenure
CCD below BQE
too small to win

reading Byrd
while getting pedi
to dwell in Hegelian doubt

& perfect naturalness
verkehrte welt
& free Chinese design

lobbed roar

a real cad compadre
crowing over limpid stars
racks up nice racks
over bubble tea's
hitting the sauce
with Pisa gum on shoe
thou naughty cloak
domicile naught
my imbecile pendulum
ambled ahead again
devouring space & time
attributed to squidy
sperm packs turgid bullet
points a signal lamp
for last remains
languished in clover
for want of sky
benediction

Grand Master van Rensselaer

I love this American Elm
dying avenues lined
with guerilla genitals
schwa assed message
on the march in March
'tits & kings
babycake IOU

hemline of colloquial
a cut above the knee
provides potlatch of porch
oily air & fungi spore
breath deeply this age
of fever & ague
veiled black smoke
bottled for poison

schools of plundered
bait fish struggle
furious with current
past teeming hum
simian affections dredge
echo from clotted muck

Pangea neurons renewed
by crow bones & tender skin
Northern Lights tattooed
on palace of luminous flesh
euphoria infested with
guileless lily ungilded
a show of hands please
for curio purposes only

mossbonkers

you   whoever you are
clenched expanse
behold the bee
divine & inevitable
lucky throat meet mandible
flicker convergence limitless
chasm descends
for eternal purports of sweat
enter your piqued aura flare
here & prepare to depart
all the haunts of wing myself

blackeye vs. monicle

we're all bosoms on the bus
Ro echoes
through the altar
of the longest color's
gauzy light to share
saffron sky above

epilates vs. epiphany
infinity pool break up's
faux paw prints
down   down   down

DB Cooper Valentine

"...it took more than one man to change my name to Shanghai Lily."

"Qui peut dire où vont les fleurs?"
chiaroscuro bouquet
of Cretan crocus
in the grotto of octopus
up in smoke
in the dark
firefly haze under adepts robe
glow worm's labyrinth
huffing Cleopatra's "dirty" bath

shanghaied venus'
poached chagrin
Bronze age all in
don't know what you're saying
but don't say it again

minor card toreador

No-Legs-Cagey
a minor despot
amends fighting words inert rocket
a lesser deck die out

oracle of disgrace
cat's eye marble trade
for Mr. Vertigo's pride

Bartelby's Wall Street
no way ichiban
platinum all the way
I prefer not to
that couch is my bitch
like if Pound rewrote the Breakfast Club

Margaretha Ebner, a Dominican nun in the mid 1300's began to miraculously lactate after a small statue of the Christ-child asked her to nurse him. Performed in accordance with her will, her heart was removed upon death and placed in a raised enamel gold reliquary, topped by a crown of lily and clover.

Ostreidae crassostrea virginica

remnant oyster cellars
owned by freed slaves
filled with oyster wenches
all of one kind
eating the sea

reverend judges & juvenile delinquents
pious & devout hypocrites
undisguised libertines & debauchees
gamblers & fancy men
high flyers & spoonies
make pickle back promises
for genteel pickpockets
on sugar factory shores

manahac-tanienk
shortened to Manhattan
means "place of inebriation"

porch minks
none of a kind
meets the one
his politics were 99% pole dancer
her politics were mostly panties
& slowly poisoned spouses

no hickies for fishing trips
just stinky select & boy butter
shave down your crime scene
to sleep with the fishes
and cook them later
cukoo coccyx
vestigial tail

No Rabbits Just Hats

for Dave Brinks

shortcut the Pegasus Parade
when the world's on fire
tailed & gilled for next life want

we were mistaken
Tasmanians are all dead
but the devil's alive
in Janine's topless Tweety tattoo
All Saint's stacked
twin bonfires (known & unknown)
for wilde beestes soldered
in a state of grace

prank mask feast
guising kid jubileed as evil ditto
for dogback martyrs & text confessors
kick that Geechie ass bird cage
in habanera 2/4 beat
for Mr.Feather's cakewalk in the sky

our limp corsage on sale
by last chance lilies
sail on silver girl sail on by
another fine mess delayed
by aural rites
dying upward
doesn't go anywhere
but away

reckoner rapture in resuscitation bay

ER doc tells me there's
a lot of machetes in Brooklyn
groove on car service
proudly incapable
of grooming one's own feet
periphery obscurity
appetite zenith
bared neck economics
a satellite stripper's nadir
prophets of aberration
she said it was too spanish
nebulous minion
penumbra jubilation
radiohead doubter
altar tipped over by
Buck Hunter video
fancy of headstone sentiment
orbiting manufacture
something attendant
especially: country adjacent

idyll deal

for Brenda Coultas

night capped mind tricks
(velvet hammer drinks
not what you think- jedi)
 back-to-school two-for-one
winged earrings unveiled
between weaning & waxing

aura ides venator's
unquenchable gams
navigate haptic figure
eights keep adding up
happenchance fatwa
stymies signifier
by blank check BFF

levy paid in peck pint or pound
Marxist landmark beneath
Guantanamera's
wonderment overflow
sexting sonnets
getting all probono on me

mall everlasting

quinta essentia
consume vampire trademark
turn the moon   on
& enter   day for night
shot in 0%
introductory
rates   all stake & sunlight

vulgar conjure
vlad fad gone mad
with mall etiquette
pet 'tit rex ©
everlasting

Water of Fail

my dear lady disdain
callipygian clam bake
slag élan
speak hands for me
to ring the bear bell
on a Darger cloud day

frutti di mare
too little too late
a goner
searing steer clear
redux influx
Wonderwheel remakes
ants in my plants- 1939
casting redoubled for
Balzac bumper cars
hinged on dicey harangue

baby-wire on Robot Alice
line-ups face it
eyes can lie
bird voyeur coffee pressed
for Albany communiqué
Jovie sighs
at B-sides

keep finding playing cards
on the street - yesterday - 9 of hearts
Cor Cordium snatched
whole from the pyre
nearly, almost
fighting a shadow

nigh your skylark
amplitudes alight
in the light
play on the wing
longing torniquet

invisible thread
baying to breath
nothing of him that doth fade
but doth suffer a sea-change
into something rich and strange
mere oblivion,
sans teeth, sans eyes, sans taste, sans everything.

Blowhole Blowhole give me back my cow

skies lacking any ambition
help consult her caul
fragments of smirk & messages
attached to migratory birds
fishnets dress up mundane thigh
of post agrarian monogamist
with statistically shrinking balls

        let me enter your sacred grove
        what thou lovest well
        remains of the day-glow ovaries

childrens' toys burned &
seen by birds of prey with
peregrine patience for
ordinary sparrows

religio
religare: to tie

Ar-the transference of a conditional curse-through the intervention of a saint
the rite of Ar is accompanied with a petition.
A saint is "tied" with a piece of cloth
until the saint complies they are tied to that spot.

**in memoriam, for David
through hearing in the Bardo**

overhead lessons begin with a thud
advanced ballroom dancing and beginner tai chi
at this very moment
thus gone
raven yidam
with four faces
a soldier's vision
in Brooklyn or Dak Tao
on the Mamaki or Delaware
dwelling in the ten directions
with the five kinds of eyes
from here to the other shore
entering existence after existence
to go on alone
in a refuge on a pathway
whatever you see
recognize it as luminosity
the wide-eyed
radiance of your own mind
emptiness cannot be harmed
by emptiness in the round cavities
left by lotus flowers as
a dewdrop sun
slips into the sea
thus gone

idyll of indigenous expressions

blueprints in snow
won't let you know
how it'll go
starling tears and pundit foes
unfriend adjuncts
sharp as a bag of wet mice

moths pinned in parlor
her mentor was a two fisted drinker
turned two time filmmaker

Thai sexpat's pop songs
another folk song lost to lipgloss
local gods eagerly await their spit take

prophet's highlight the disaster montage
botany in the foreground
serves up tonic while
fire tunnel opens to ocean

girls in company of shadows
upheld hope with light
hot kiss from a bruised fist
nobody's pet that snake
wants his gland back

PART III

CONTAGION

An effect resembles its cause; and things which have once been in contact with each other continue to act on each other at a distance after the physical contact has been severed. The former principle may be called the Law of Similarity, the latter the Law of Contact or Contagion.

Sir James Frazer, *The Golden Bough*

Ars longa,
vita brevis,
occasio praeceps,
experimentum periculosum
iudicium difficile

see saw wound memento
negative capability panties
nitwit leanings

Cartesian spider monkey yells,
"Titans - show us your tits"
rainbow mice gaze
into ten-dimensions
& drunk dials the nimbus

expired breast milk with
lip stick stuck moth
& flesh-tone jeans

FUBAR'd sycophants
Tebowed fates beholden to
beguiled pedophile's
listening devices   in there
our ear parts   are all the same

suckle moths with wine
and truths unspoken
fortune teller crow boys
eat your heart out
so few, these days, know the game

cotillion contagion

"… *The rhythm stretches out heathenish and ragged. The quick contagion is caught by a few in the crowd, who take it up with spirited smitings of the bare sole upon the ground, and of open hands upon the thighs.*"

>Cable Sang, *The Dance in the Place Congo*
>*The Century Magazine,* February 1886

river escaped
rolled up into sky
the song has changed
mated & frantic
response calling
in vehement mire
smitten bared sole
on ground snatched
sonorous rising from oblivion
contagion in unison
putting on airs &
French corrupted on thick tongues

trick day

raptor robber of eggs
hollowed from dragon eyes
wish-command star-fade
into authentic mockingbird mock-down
gloam stirred silhouette
by flame-licked lion
hollow form of pelvis fused to shell
extrinsic's unwitting alms

above Thai arrows' gold
woefully inadequate
in between pawed curtain
almost a place or season
offers hip bath inherited by lightning
in a distant gateless future

she who whispers

for Megan Burns

mopping it Catholic
with perfume muddled
graveyard dust promises
blood is so interior

crooked crow wavers
in crowned head clouds
sky becomes emoticon irony
contemplation of the beardless
beset in mourning attire's
youth dervish

play pretend till the play's real
moth to taper
smoke obscured sightline
witness play's bayou boy
full of doubt

is a chaos

bedeviling bias
with owl malaise
tail feather skeleton
resides inside the mask
astride cap of feathers
made unreal
in domain of revelation
shamanizing sensation
of actual flight
making it holy & choked in blood
bridge manifesting skin

on the run

bourbon swill sidelined
by Caravaggio hoi polloi
barefoot in chapel
behind faded scrim
nave of postcard
conjuring trick
declines to reveal
your filthy feet lovingly painted

caster catcher
builds gallows low
just on principle
to inhabit clouds
the shape of question marks

Saint Expedite

horse shoe's protection
overlooked

annunciation
winged uterine mimic

machine à faire autre
vaporous factories rise

veneer of predatory stare
this lowly vital pulse

hardening wings
in locust's final molt

ghosts envied goose
avatar of Christmas past

The worship of this folk saint takes the form of a syncretic cult, mixing unofficial Catholicism with other beliefs. The usual iconography shows a Roman foot soldier holding a clock marked "Hodie"(Today) and stepping on a raven who beckons "Cras"(Tomorrow).

this was a person it seems

shorn crow
with larger sense of stone
bereft of dawn

& darkness settles in
medium of wind
vortice of white owl's warning
born from forehead
intent desire
in abundance

above anemones

yolk eclipsed sun
bruised elbow in the spaghetti western
let's make the script up as we go along
do some dying today
can't afford blood pellets
but falling in slow motion
worth   every   penny

Miss Mary Mack Mack Mack dressed in black black black
With silver buttons buttons buttons down her back back back
He jumped so high, high, high
He reached the sky, sky, sky
He never came back, back, back
'Til the 4th of July, ly, ly
bamboo invades meadow
colonial rhizome & wheat fields nod
adieu adieu to you & you & you
Uturi drain pipe on gas land river
golden rod into knot weed
& purple loose strife crowds
Fourth of July forget-me-nots
the day he died I didn't know him yet

braided hair & fuck you shirt
Bernadette's beams sistered with scraps
Dave couldn't remember all his kid's names
tree suckers not enough light
blind owl in reptile throat
limbic eyes dart past iambic lines
buddleia tied to tricycle
where they put the cemetery
across the brick face
under power plant parrot
nests nineteenth century plots
similar to corn fields'
simulated pastoral
Pekinese ducks too fat to fly or fail

glide to a stop & song begins again
how long does nostalgia take?
the swiss illness: a memory unfolded
reveals several other knives
carousel of minor spoon & fork
these attachments stowed
in knife's pivot point
coat of arms gilded pacifier

blasphemed redeemer
of disrupted landscape
pitches postcard new
reminds you to go home
to a place you've just arrived
little tic let's her know
lucky hand next time
wake up hogtied
name chewed into feathered cap
worn with malochia to covet
thick minds my lilies are obscene
please irrigate the weeds while I am away
only half the ocean died this year
get your tiny monkey eyes off my big monkey head

goods unlimited

for George Foster

it's snowing
on the wing
of Project virgin in relief
by Brooklyn borealis

folk lullaby in karaoke bar
taboos & tattoos
for draconian
measures amok

silkworm's contrails expanded
out to shipping containers
filled with frogs

the future and the dead
split apart as two
long gone & still here
grey river reflects
& begets new cargo

malochia of want unblinking
finite wells look and see brides
in blue something
appeased to faith servers'
religion in the wheat
below broken knees & curbs
the great American sunset
in oily street puddle
look- a rainbow

falsely entitled soccer fans

for Jovah McLemore

beak to beak amalgam
in abandoned factory
Corvallis corvid's heart
of the valley nerve

first matter hand tremors
gesturer closes hand
getting lucky
with a variety of silk moths

Egyptian blue inquires
on the causes of roots
the future's permanent beta
sooner & stranger
than you think

something around the eyes'
elusive shadow
with gaze luminescence
striking down & inward
underpainting the deceased

traiteuse

under the light of fire flies
a kind of ferning occurs
pumpkin sky presses
water marked arm buds

bend a finer canvas better to fly
with lime sized human intact
each star forgotten
under your cast an itch

moss & feathers sewn up
for today's no-no's
unable to run
but mind still races
light to optic nerve & retina
a blind spot where
I left you a note
containing one word

crop milk for squab

for Allison Cobb

"…Where would I be if I lost my pal
Fifteen miles on the Erie Canal
I'd like to see a mule good as my Sal…"

we begin the story again
except this time in Portland
she couldn't sleep knowing
the street trees all needed water

they began dredging the Hudson
to find the body of a famed moth specialist
disconnected from the living
in the midst of a mass extinction
a noxious species invasion
entirely unaware everywhere
find an organism to get a sense of it
it's luxuriate selfness
all around you
the emptiness is still opening up
the pale space between each of us
within our very molecules

our meandering was over
owls mad with captivity-rage
devoted ally of bugs and wobblies
hope fashioned with peanut butter effigies
flinging out the nothingness
gone to smithereens

live feed of cemetery

a shaman faux paux
revealed by freelance wizards
as the exorcist ends his exercise
they say the soothsayer
never knew what hit her
a seer signs up for a superbowl pool

salt over shoulder
where past and future may mingle
in empty sky flown
out beyond inert now

a catapult to the fox world
those devils not held to a pack
reads relief fragments in temple of eyes
whispered instructions in landscape disruptions

Ishtar's handshake and Kitsune's wink
blister symptoms of this
veiled more or less
with foxy promises

Dem Tod ein Paar Schuhe schenken

to have given death a pair of shoes-an old German expression for having escaped death

on the gossip recon to find Pete's wife
she's somewhere out there far away
inside the old story of
I don't really love you, so much

we almost forgot even Sharon
had a hit once with broken socks
& compulsive mythmaking a
not-entirely-requited love affair
corresponding projections
languishing away with faux verite visions
no bigger than a grain of barley
indistinct but the blood
stirs with manifest priest's destiny
mandatory baptism & scientific fatalism
oh to die with your shoes on
and never know what hit you

Scalapino vs. Barbarino

for Molly Dorozenski

mystery plumbed
in rapacious mine
metal lust   flecked into
eroded gully   gold sluice's precious
gaping porch of gash land
mercury salesman sternum-deep
with seduced pollinators
four salts collected
for deep packet inspection
compass rose bloom's
wild grass swath
peopled by convicts & bastards
anointed 'A' & accepted penance
to embroider shame
of paranormal D cup

Magic deals with impersonal forces, and aims at control or constraint, not conciliation... as religion would do. For it assumes that all personal beings, whether human or divine are subject to those impersonal forces which control all things... The operation of immutable laws acting mechanically, [magic is in essence] the bastard sister of science... Both magic and science assume the succession of events is perfectly regular and certain being determined by immutable laws, the operation of which can be foreseen and calculated precisely.

-Sir James Frazer, *The Golden Bough*

aqua e sali

soco fanno limaari
non chi pozza giovaro
malochia whatsoever
thrown where none may walk
careful not to say amen
variant of drunk
befalls mischief's
blessed eternity
such pervasive multitude of tiny eyes
every bird in Scotland and elsewhere
with tides of innumerable amen

ladyboy lullaby

conceal austerity turns-ons
for agave war story
told shot by shot
in whim fusion's
lingual stagger

echo layered in coup collusion
of two worlds bounced back
with gimlet-eyed entrancement
a send-up of sign-offs for
slip-ups in middle path muddled

solicit tension & initiate mysteries
extraction talisman's
oculas mentis
so bereft of sense

book of whore hours

snake bite invokes knot magic
a satyr's fauna reduction
remembers dismembered lovers (kindly)

nectar king forgets
sticky calendar notes
to summon rain today
the truck-fallen sale buys
carnival's farewell to flesh
from lifted carnie meat

navigum isidis
lost & owl eyed
tip toe into vortex

King Momo on fire
in the house of bees
declining growth

migrant labor overlooks
obsidian knife
in future's back

uncouth godlette
appeased in inky shadow
decay into regeneration
serpent moistened
tentacles unfurled with spade
celestial veil's same-same
star of cock block melancholic

Aurora Consurgens

pharmakon portent's
elixir of beginning
both remedy & poison

hotwinged blood
refrains from breath
for papyri theft
& time-mocked corpus

sextricate yourself now
from estrogen crazy train
& double park hearse with
with tiger teet mourning
dead arm's milk cookies

Fool's Gold exorcism
charms death's tongue
luting the joints
hidden on the hip
with Old Crow flask's
glinting light

unctuous decline

1% of the 99%
are aware of the 1%
pearls' evidence of pain
Cyprian charms for
shot caller refund
in the cave
& on the foam

wonder why lies lassoed
for headcase's tongue twister
pulls petals love-me-nots
eked out questions

get your diabetes socks over here
getting into back seat
fairly early these days

cestus messed us up
He hath awakened
from the dream of life
such invulnerable nothings

Incunabula

Vinculum quippe vinculorum amor est

lost in soul-stamped
soapy ascent & knee-tangle
temple snakes licked
her ears clean
so she could hear
future breath made audible
as stars fade & dinosaur discovers flight
scales sprout feathers
& lights converge
now now now & then

Ein Sof Ayin

clave sticks serve
as decoder rings
to cipher music
timing is something
but not always everything

underscore the score
head bonk stars in orbit
cartoon of pupils dilate
breath deep or not at all

double secret probation

potential infinities rubberbanded
a perfect fifth
redials rebirth
cartographer caress
tells you   you are here
forget maps   get lost in your own kitchen
vinculum scream of light
outlasted stars &
cosmic background hiss

the sky has writing on it
rifle muzak watches
over me & above enemies
a zero ring trade-off
aortic knot throb
double bloom Twombly
pipevine swallowtail's
infinite poison to mimic my sweet

can't hide trembling WTF bliss
courtly bourbon bullet
insists hope is for suckers
(knowing) the bends rule
of thumbing a ride with bubbles
& come out terra terrified
stumble-foot so inadequate
after swimming in finned footed abyss

Tracey McTague lives up on Battle Hill in Brooklyn, down the street from where she was born and across the room from where her daughter was born. She is the ornithologist consigliere for *Lungfull! Magazine* by day. By night, she is a root doctor, alchemist and hunter-gatherer.

Titles from Trembling Pillow Press

I of the Storm by Bill Lavender

Olympia Street by Michael Ford

Ethereal Avalanche by Gina Ferrara

Transfixion by Bill Lavender

The Ethics of Sleep by Bernadette Mayer

Downtown by Lee Meitzen Grue

SONG OF PRAISE   *Homage To John Coltrane* by John Sinclair

Untitled Writings From A Member of the Blank Generation by Philip Good

DESERT JOURNAL by ruth weiss

Aesthesia Balderdash by Kim Vodicka

Of Love & Capital by Christopher Rizzo (Winner of the 2012 Bob Kaufman Book Prize, selected by Bernadette Mayer)

SUPER NATURAL by *Tracey McTague*

Forthcoming Titles

I LOVE THIS AMERICAN WAY OF LIFE by Brett Evans

loaded arc by Laura Goldstein

Full Tilt Boogie or What's The Point by Paul Chasse

Trembling Pillow
PRESS

Website: http://www.tremblingpillowpress.com

Made in the USA
Charleston, SC
13 March 2013